A GUIDE TO HOPI
KATSINA
CARVINGS

Western National Parks Association
Tucson, Arizona

Published by Western
National Parks Association

The net proceeds from WNPA publica-
tions support education and research pro-
grams in the national parks. To learn
more, visit www.wnpa.org.

Written by Rose Houk
Edited by Abby Mogollón
Designed by Mo Martin
Photography by George H. H. Huey
Printing by Imago

Cover carving by Branden Kayquaptewa
Title page carving by Gerold Hayah
Carving page 5 by Lawrence Acadiz

Special thanks to Kaibab Courtyard
Shops and Silver Bell Trading for loaning
WNPA several of the katsinam pictured
in this book.

And thanks to Bill Beaver, Steve Beiser,
and Steve Pickle for their time and
expertise.

Printed in China

Cataloging-in-Publication data on file

CONTENTS

INTRODUCTION

From winter solstice until midsummer each year, the benevolent spirits called *katsinam* live among the Hopi on their three mesas in northern Arizona. The katsinam, central to Hopi religion, are given form as wooden carvings popularly known as "kachina dolls."

The Hopi believe that the carvings, or *tithu*, are made by the katsinam themselves in their own likenesses. The figures were, and still are, given to Hopi females of all ages and to infant boys.

The earliest Anglo collectors of the carvings were U.S. Army surgeons who came to Hopi in the 1850s. Though some Hopi resisted selling what are essentially religious objects, by the early twentieth century katsina carvings were being made and sold more widely. Today, many Hopi make a good living selling their carvings. (Other Pueblo people, notably the Zuni, also produce katsina figures.)

Traditional katsina carvings were simple forms without a base, carved by hand, sanded with a stone, and painted with natural pigments. Also called cradle dolls, these are the first carvings a young child receives. They are made to be hung on the wall.

In the early 1900s shapes grew more complex and three-dimensional. After World War II, figures began to show action—knees bent, a foot raised, an arm outstretched. More detail was added, and commercial paints lent brighter colors. At the urging of traders, carvers placed the pieces on wood bases and signed them on the bottom. Later, carvers introduced contemporary sculptural forms, each made from a single piece of wood with intricate detail accomplished with electric carving tools. In the 1970s, however, this trend was countered by a return to the older style carvings. Some carvers who have adopted this "new" traditional style feel the figures better capture the true spirit of the katsinam.

Hopi men traditionally are the carvers, and individuals develop distinctive styles. That style, some say, can best be seen in the hands and feet of the figure; others discern it in the choice of paints and colors. The root of the cottonwood tree is the preferred material, but as it has become scarcer around the mesas carvers have had to go farther afield to get it. Other woods have been tried, but none have replaced *paako,* cottonwood root. A carver's tools usually are simple— pocket knife, chisel, X-acto knife, and sandpaper— though Dremel drills and woodburning tools have come into use as well.

For paints, mineral and vegetable pigments gathered from the land are traditional, but many carvers now use poster paints and acrylics. Katsina carvings often are adorned with fur, yarn, cloth, and feathers. Eagle, hawk, and owl feathers were used until federal laws prohibited possession or resale of any part of these protected birds. Carvers have adapted, substituting detailed carving or feathers of domestic birds.

The best advice for collecting is to buy carvings that attract you, either for their craftsmanship and beauty or for the meaning behind them. Much to the displeasure of the Hopi, there is a lively business in mass-produced, factory-made pieces by non-Hopi. To assure getting an authentic carving, buy directly from a Hopi carver if possible, or from a known, reputable dealer such as a museum shop or an experienced trader.

Hopi katsina carvings will likely continue to reflect the personal styles of the artists and the tastes of the market. Yet even as carvings evolve, they will always possess enduring meaning as symbols of something much greater: the Hopi way of life.

KATSINAM CEREMONIES

Around winter solstice, the ceremonial chambers called *kivas* are opened in the villages and the paths are laid out to usher in the katsinam, whom the Hopi beseech for good health, prosperity, fertility, growth, and specifically, water. In rituals practiced for at least a thousand years, men put on full costume with masks and perform dances. They personify the various katsinam, serving as tangible manifestations of the intangible spirits.

During these six months from winter solstice until midsummer, a series of significant ceremonies, some lasting for many days and nights, take place within the kivas and in the outdoor plazas of the villages. The first katsina of the season appears at winter solstice, a time of fasting and prayer when the Sun is called back from its northward journey. Two other major katsina ceremonial periods occur, one in February, called *Powamuya* or Bean Dance, the other in mid-July, known as Home Dance or *Niman*.

The day after Niman, the katsina season officially closes. All the katsinam depart for the San Francisco Peaks and a few other neighboring locations, where they will spend the other half of the year. The one exception is Masaw, the supreme deity on this earth who gave the Hopi their land, along with fire and agriculture. He stays among the Hopi and may appear at any time of year.

Though it's uncertain exactly how many Hopi katsinam exist, there may be 300 to as many as 500. The number isn't fixed. New ones are introduced and old ones fall away through the years; also, most do not appear at every village or on every mesa each year. Those illustrated here were chosen to give a sample of the various categories and rich diversity of the katsinam. ✤

SOLSTICE KATSINA
— Soyal

The arrival of Soyal at winter solstice opens the katsina season on Third Mesa each year. He walks slowly upon emergence, as if elderly or just awakened from a long sleep. Soyal stumbles and weaves while the people reach out to help him stay upright. He sings in a low, weak voice as he sprinkles cornmeal and places prayer feathers, or pahos, at a kiva. Soyal is the one who taught the Hopi the art of making pahos.

He wears a white cotton shirt, leggings, and a blanket, with a twist of black yarn over his right shoulder. His hands are painted with white zigzags—in one hand he carries a sack of meal and four prayer sticks and in the other a gourd rattle. A gourd-shaped topknot tufted with horsehair and a feather are distinguishing features.

ARTIST: *Lawrence Acadiz*

KATSINA GRANDMOTHER
— Hahay'i wuuti

Katsina Grandmother, or Happy Mother, shares with Crow Mother the title of mother of all the katsinam. Hahay'i wuuti's husband is said to be Eototo or Chaveyo, and her children are the monsters, the Nataskas.

Appearing during the Bean Dance, or Powamuya, and at other important ceremonies, she speaks in a high voice and is very talkative. She assumes many guises in various ceremonies, sometimes demanding meat for the Nataskas or giving bread to children. This katsina is also known as Pour Water Woman because she often pours water over the heads of spectators.

Hahay'i wuuti wears a white mask with a single feather on top and has a red spot on each cheek. Her hairstyle is that of a traditional Hopi female, with side whorls and bangs. Clothing is a dress, belt, moccasins, and maiden's shawl.

Flat carvings of Hahay'i wuuti are given to Hopi infants. As a young girl matures, she receives larger, more detailed forms.

ARTIST: Horace Kayquoptewa

11

CROW MOTHER
— *Angwusnasomtaka*

Crow Mother is the mother of the Hu, or Whipper Katsinam. She appears during Powamuya to oversee the children's initiation into the katsina religion. Carrying yucca whips or a basket of corn kernels or fresh bean sprouts, Crow Mother leads other katsinam into the village with great dignity. The name Angwusnasomtaka means "one who has crow feathers tied to it." The winglike appendages coming out of either side of her head are a trademark, as are the green face and green moccasins.

Powamuya, or Bean Dance, is a series of ceremonies that takes place over many days in February. The emphasis is purification. When the katsinam come out of the kivas with freshly sprouted bean seeds and corn stalks, it is a sign of a good harvest even though the land is still locked in winter.

Along with Crow Mother comes an elaborate procession of katsina dancers including Dawn and Imitator katsinam, various Ogres, clowns, and a host of others.

ARTIST: *Derek Hayah*

EOTOTO

Eototo is the father, or chief, of all katsinam. He is familiar with all the ceremonies and controls the seasons. On Third Mesa, he appears at Powamuya with Aholi, a lieutenant of sorts. (On First and Second Mesas he appears without Aholi.) Some carvers portray Eototo and Aholi as individual figures, while others will pair these two.

Eototo conducts the ceremony to bring clouds and rain. He draws a cloud symbol on the ground, upon which Aholi places his staff and roars a call. Aholi then repeats everything else Eototo does, following him as he administers blessings and pours sacred water. In contrast to the unadorned, nearly all-white figure of Eototo, Aholi is dressed elaborately in a colorful cloak, cone-shaped blue mask, and other adornments.

Eototo is also part of Niman, or Home Dance, which concludes the katsina cycle each year.

ARTIST: *Duane Hyeoma*

OGRE WOMAN
— *Soyoko wuuti*

Ogre Woman first appears suddenly on a winter evening during Powamuya. She goes house-to-house disciplining children, demanding that young boys catch mice and game, and that girls grind corn and prepare sacred foods. She presents a terrifying aspect—black face with wild hair, a black dress, and a cane. Hooting and wailing, Ogre Woman threatens to eat the children if she is not satisfied.

When she returns to each home, she brings others in her family along with her. They growl, brandish frightening knives or cleavers, and act as if they are ready to carry the children away. The ogres demand tribute but often turn down the offerings.

But as with many katsina ceremonies, there is a message or an object lesson in how to live the proper Hopi way. When Ogre Woman and her sidekicks come to the dance, they are driven away because of their greed.

ARTIST: *Duane Hyeoma*

BROAD FACE
— *Wuyak kuita*

Also called Big Head, Broad Face is a
Hu, or Whipper, katsina. His role is to
maintain discipline and make sure spectators honor Powamuya ceremonies. Broad
Face has also been the one to assure that
necessary village work is accomplished
each year.

Moving with heavy steps, Broad Face
is a rather fearful figure, with long beard,
two curved horns, and eyes that pop out
of his face. He brings up the end of the
line of dancers, keeping everyone moving
with yucca whips. On First Mesa, he
appears with Ogre Woman.

ARTIST: *Lawrence Yellowhair*

19

SNOW KATSINA GIRL

— *Nuvakchin Mana*

As the name suggests, Snow Katsina Girl represents snow. She is often at Niman. Though Niman is in summer, the Hopi look ahead and ask for cold weather to come with the accompanying moisture that will replenish the soil for next year's planting.

Snow Katsina Girl has a white face and hair, and sometimes she is carved kneeling and playing a gourd rasp.

Though there are many female, or maiden, katsinam, men are the ones who do the personations at the dances.

ARTIST: *Paqua Group*

LONG-HAIRED KATSINA

— Angaktsina

The long-haired katsina is a dancer and a singer of sweet songs who brings rain and flowers. This is one of the most widely distributed katsinam, popular among the Zuni and Rio Grande pueblos as well.

The long-haired katsina's beard and loose tresses symbolize rain and clouds. This katsina manifests itself in different forms, such as barefoot or lightning long-haired katsina.

Long-hairs appear as a group at Niman and at plaza dances with maidens.

ARTIST: *Eric Kayquaptewa*

NAVAJO
— *Tasap*

Certain katsinam represent other tribes, such as Navajo, Apache, Comanche, and Zuni. These carvings are not made by or borrowed from other Indians but are Hopi representations of their neighbors.

Tasap is dressed as a Navajo dancer but has some birdlike characteristics as well, such as a long beaked nose. A group of them forms a line in village plaza dances in the springtime, moving slowly to a heavy beat. Tasap are often joined by the Navajo Katsina Girl.

ARTIST: *Lawrence Acadiz*

25

JÉMEZ OR
RIPENED CORN KATSINA
— Hemis

Like the Navajo Tasap, Hemis is a katsina inspired by another group—this one the Jémez people who live in northern New Mexico. Hemis brings the first harvest of whole ripe corn plants at Niman. He also carries gifts tied to cornstalks, some of which brides will receive. These katsinam enter the plaza at sunrise, forming double lines and wearing great *tablitas* as part of their masks. They move and turn with the maidens in a complex, beautiful dance.

Niman lasts sixteen days, all of it taking place in kivas except for the final day. On that day, the katsinam appear in public for the last time before they return to the San Francisco Peaks. At the end of Niman, the Katsina Father says to them: "Now go back home happily, but do not forget us. Come to visit us as rain. That is all."

ARTIST: *Leo Lacapa*

CHILI

— Tsil

Chili is one of the runner, or racer, katsinam that challenge men and boys to foot races during the spring dances. When so challenged, a man begins at a starting line with the racer katsinam in hot pursuit. Winners receive prizes, but losers are humiliated in public by the racers. Chili forces hot peppers into the loser's mouth; other katsinam rub soot, grease, and mud on the opponent.

Chili has a yellow face, and as with most runners has large round eyes and wears scant clothing for freer movement. Chili gets paid in piki, the traditional wafer-thin bread made with blue cornmeal on a hot stone.

ARTIST: *Lawrence Acadiz*

EAGLE
— *Kwahu*

The eagle katsina appears most often at kiva dances in March. It enacts the motions of eagles, hoping to increase numbers of these most significant birds. To the Hopi, eagles are guests. They are given gifts and they symbolically carry on their backs prayers for a good world.

The Hopi have several other bird katsinam, including crow, duck, quail, parrot, hummingbird, and roadrunner.

ARTIST: *Ron Koopee*

31

GREAT HORNED OWL
— Mongwu

Another bird katsina, Great Horned Owl is the leader of the raider, or warrior, katsinam. He constantly combats the clowns or disciplines them if they become too rowdy.

Great Horned Owl quietly enters the plaza. He stands back and watches the clowns for a time, departs, then reappears hooting and edging closer to the clowns. Joined by other raiders, he finally jumps on the clowns as punishment for their non-Hopi behavior.

Like Eagle, Great Horned Owl is a favored carving, with plentiful feathers, fur, and wood. Birds and their feathers play important roles in pueblo stories. They are valued for their instruction, advice, and help. Some birds were desired for trade, others because of their association with water.

ARTIST: *Derek Hayah*

BEAR
— Hon

One of the most important roles of animal katsinam is to heal disease and illness. Bear is imbued with this great power.

He appears in different colors including blue, black, white, and yellow. A bear footprint on the cheek, long snout, and bared teeth distinguish this katsina.

Bears are significant in Hopi history. In the old days, families and friends traveled together as the Hopi migrated into this, the Fourth World. One group came upon a dead bear, taking it as a sign that they would be known as the Bear Clan. Many other clans then developed, each continuing to move until settling finally in the villages on the three mesas where the Hopi live today.

In addition to Bear, the Hopi have a rich roster of other animal katsinam, including deer, antelope, wolf, and ram. They consider animals their closest neighbors; when approached respectfully with cornmeal and prayer feathers, the animals will aid them.

ARTIST: *Horace Kayquoptewa*

BADGER
— *Honan*

Like Bear, Badger is also a healer, an influential one because he knows all the valuable medicinal roots and herbs. In one form, Badger appears on Second Mesa during Powamuya with tracks on his cheeks; in other forms he is seen in mixed dances.

There is also a Badger Clan among the Hopi. When they first arrived near the mesas, their camp was surrounded by flowers even though it was winter. So, they were granted permission to stay at the village of Old Oraibi.

All the animal katsinam, says scholar Barton Wright, possess the unique ability to take off their skins and hang them up, appearing as men in the kivas and carrying on normal conversations.

ARTIST: *Timothy Talawepi*

SPOTTED OR SPECKLED CORN
— *Avachhoya*

Corn katsinam are popular, common spirits because corn is the supreme Hopi food. Hopi author Alph Secakuku says, "Corn is sacred; it is life; it is Hopi." Spotted Corn is the younger brother of Hemis, and young boys often impersonate this one at dances. This katsina can appear in several versions, though all have feathers on the head pointing toward the four directions and often have spots all over the body. During their lively dance, they function to aid corn production.

Some varieties of corn are planted as early as April at Hopi, attended by specific rituals. By June, when the weather has warmed, farmers put more corn into the fields. After harvest, it is stacked in homes and used in a number of dishes throughout the year.

ARTIST: *Branden Kayquaptewa*

39

SQUASH

— *Patung*

The Hopi gather and grow a wide array of both wild and cultivated plants. Squash, along with corn and beans, makes up the harmonious trio of traditional cultivated foods.

Squash is an important katsina for the Pumpkin Clan. He appears on First Mesa as a runner. Collectors like this one and it is often carved, with striped body and head in a squash-like shape.

Plant katsinam bring their own water. As dry farmers, dependent on 10 to 18 inches of precipitation that comes each year, the Hopi value highly any katsina that comes bearing moisture.

ARTIST: *Carl Bahnimptewa*

41

CRICKET
— Su söpa

Several insects and reptiles are represented among the katsinam: scorpion, bee, hornet, and water serpent among them. Though many katsinam hold gourd rattles, ears of corn, and staffs in their hands, Cricket usually doesn't carry anything when he dances except piki bread at times.

He wears a kilt and a black bandolier, and he sports tufts of feathers instead of ears.

The Hopi honor insects with important, powerful roles in their ceremonies.

ARTIST: Leroy Pooley

MUDHEAD
— Koyemsi

Mudheads are a complex collection and serve many functions in katsina ceremonies. They lead dances, drum, sing, play games, distribute seeds, and battle clowns. For some dances, they form a chorus. A pair of mudheads announces the beginning of the night kiva dances in March, and during foot races a mudhead carries prizes in a blanket. They are also considered curers and the messengers between humans and the supernaturals. Hopi say that mudheads are the offspring of incestuous unions, which accounts for their grotesque appearance and underscores the results of improper behavior.

The nickname "mudhead" is not a Hopi term but arises from the ochre mud applied to their sack masks and bodies.

One interesting version depicts a blind mudhead carrying a paralyzed man, Tuhavi, on his back. These two were left behind during a disaster, and Tuhavi became the mudhead's eyes, helping both to survive.

ARTIST: *Fred Chapella*

CLOWNS
— *Koyaalam, Tsuku*

Because they do not wear masks, clowns are not real katsinam. They sometimes appear with the katsinam, or take over while the katsinam are resting.

Clowns serve as irreverent comedians, mocking the behavior of spectators, especially Anglos. They sometimes engage in risque acts that arouse uproarious laughter among spectators. The clowns are warned to correct their un-Hopilike behavior, but ignoring the warnings they are then punished. The clowns' role, says trader Jonathan Day, is to show "how not to be Hopi."

The figures are shown doing everything from eating watermelon to shooting basketballs. They are painted yellow or in black-and-white stripes.

ARTIST: *Regina NaHa*

GLOSSARY

KATSINA (PL. KATSINAM)—a benevolent spirit being; participant in a katsina ceremony; and a representative wooden carving

KIVA—a partially underground chamber in pueblo villages, where katsina and other ceremonies are held. Kivas are roofed and entered down a ladder.

MANA—maiden

NIMAN—Home Dance, takes place on Hopi Mesas in mid-July each year; marks end of the katsina season

PAAKO—cottonwood root, traditional preferred material for katsina carvings

POWAMUYA—Bean Dance, in early February on Hopi Mesas, first major katsina ceremony of year

TABLITA—headdress in the form of a plaque decorated with feathers and symbolic designs

TIHU (PL. TITHU)—wooden katsina carving

WUUTI—female